# Tips to Unlocking
# the
# Book Within You

## Kathie Walters

**Tips to Unlocking the Book Within You**

ISBN- 978-1-888081-81-7

Printed in the United States of America
Published by Good News Ministries
220 Sleepy Creek Rd
Macon GA 31210

kathiewalters@mindspring.com

# Table of Contents

## Introduction

Kathie Walters believes that many people have something to say or something to tell. Now is the time to say it, because God has deposited value and a certain kind of drama in everyone's life. I believe if someone has a boring life it's because they choose to. But if you step out and do some things that are in your heart you can live in the "exciting." That's a great place to live and you will find you have things to say and places to go that will attract others. Besides that - it won't be boring.

# So, you want to write a book?

So you want to write a book, or you feel you are meant to be heard in some way? Well this is the time when God wants His people to speak up. Your story, book, testimony or teaching may not get out there to hundreds of thousands of people, but in your church, family and circle of friends there are people who would love to read your book. You can never be sure where something will go when God is involved. But you have to start somewhere or you will never know. Of course, if you are a speaker you have an advantage, because if people benefit from your teaching or speaking, they probably would like to have your book.

Nearly all genuine publishers do not accept unsolicited manuscripts for consideration. They will advise you to get a literary agent, but most genuine literary agents do not take on people's work that is unknown and unproven. Many Christians feel they have a great testimony to share, but if you write your testimony you have to stop and seriously think, "Who is going to read it?" The people you have personal contact with is the answer. It's probably not going to be on the "New York Times" best seller list. So all you really want is maybe a few hundred copies. You don't want to be required to have 2,000 to 5,000 copies printed to get a good price. If you are a speaker then you know you will have a wider audience and therefore you will reach more people and obviously sell more books. Good News for you -you don't have to order 5,000 to get a good price you can order 100 at a time or even 20 at a time.

But it's not all bad news; you just need a little help.

THIS IS FOR THOSE WHO HAVE A TESTIMONY OR STORY TO WRITE - not so much for people intending to write a technical book, reference book or theology book.

David and I have written numerous articles and about twenty-eight books between us. We also have approximately 16 sets of teaching CD's and videos. Everyone has their own style and personality. I personally believe that something of yourself should show through your work, unless it's a hindrance to the reader. A good friend of mine begins every sentence with the word, "Well....". Which is not necessarily the best idea.

# Who should write a book?

Many people say to me things like this: "I feel I am supposed to write a book." "I think I should write a book or booklet." "I would like to teach like you do, but I am not sure how to start." .

So I ask them , *"What is it that you want to write about?" "What is that you want to teach?"*

Many times they will respond with, *"I'm not really sure what I want to write about"* or, *"I'm not sure what to teach."*

I say, *"Well don't write it"* or, *"Don't teach it."* Make sure you know what it is you want to say. If it's a testimony make sure and know the points you want to bring out. Putting every detail may make it too lengthy. You  need to write with conviction.

So take a little time alone and ask yourself, *"What do I really want to say, what is it that I really want people to know?"*

What particular truth do you find yourself thinking, *"I wish everyone knew this."* That is telling you something. It is telling you what your real message is all about.

As previously indicated, very few testimony or teaching or story books  make the best sellers list. Now if you have an exceptional testimony or story, like you raised some people from the dead and walked on water, that might get some attention. To be quite honest, unless Publishers already know there is a market for you or you already have a good market yourself, they are not really interested, because guess what? They want to make money from your book.

## The Good News

But we have good news for you. Instead of spending thousands of dollars with a vanity printer, you can have 20, 50 or 100 books printed for the same price per copy as others who will pay a printer/publisher to print 3,000 or 5,000 to get a decent price.

You can do your own book with a little help and know-how, which is what we are here for. We publish our own books, because we have an outlet; you can do the same and have a similar outlet, and we can help make that happen for you. We steer clear of editing, but we can help you find an editor if needed.

What we can do is format your book for printing, set you up with an ISBN number and have your copies printed within a couple of weeks; not months like some publishers take. Most books of 150 - 200 pages are around $3.00 -$3.50 a copy to produce and you can have as few or as many as you like.

If you want to add, change or correct text after it's printed, the cost is very modest to do that. To keep the price low, the book interior must be printed in black and white, but the cover can be done in full color. And we can also supply you with various cover options. We can also make your book available as an e-book, on kindle and in Amazon and Barnes and Noble!

# Selah - think on this

Before you rush ahead, you must be able to be objective and stand back a little from your story. You have to consider the reader and how things appeal to them, because you want people to read what you are going to write.

Another good friend of our family who has been in the ministry for years and years, had a book that someone had helped him put together.

*"It has good content, but it looks homemade if you know what I mean."* I said to him.

*"Oh, well I don't care if it gets 'out there' or not."* he replied.

*"If you don't care if people read it, what's the point of writing it?"*

He was kinda caught off guard by that. So we took his book and made it into a very attractive little production. And this helped get it out there for people to read and be ministered to.

So when you are considering the reader, it's a good idea to have honest friends who will tell you the truth. Your mom probably won't, because she thinks it's great, just because you wrote it.

So bear these few things in mind when you write or think about writing and this will help write a better story or teaching.

# Don't make it too lengthy

By and large readers these days are basically lazy. That is because this is a media driven, sight-sound society. Why read a book when you can sit and watch a movie about it? So don't make your book a vast and complicated volume; 200 pages should be maximum.

Ask yourself this question. How many of you have not started a book because of its size? It was too intimidating, time consuming and challenging. How many times have you started a book and never finished it because you got bogged down? I am not talking about good fictional novels, but life stories or testimonies and teaching.

Someone sent me a book recently, asking my opinion. I've picked it up several times now and put it down again. It's very wordy and very big (to me) so I felt disheartened and tired and I'm pretty sure I will never open it.

Thirty, forty or fifty years ago, people read books and articles, because it was one of the major means of entertainment or education. I couldn't believe it one morning when I had the TV on to the education channel. The smart *"educator"* was teaching a class of kids - something about history. She told the class, *"I wouldn't bother to read the book, you can probably find a DVD."* I couldn't believe my ears. But then I guess that how it is these days. She was actually teaching them not to read.

So apart from the very few who just love reading, most people don't want to work at it. They just want to know what it is you have to say, the easiest way possible.

# Keep it simple

You can use good words, but I would keep away from long words that most people don't know the meaning of.

And remember not to repeat yourself. Sometimes when someone is eager to get a point across they keep saying the same thing over and over.

And try not to use the same word in two consecutive sentences. Keeping a good Thesaurus on hand will help with that.

You can say something serious without making it heavy, and by "heavy" I mean hard to read. If you are writing a serious teaching, and there is a way to put something humorous in, do it, especially if you can say something funny about yourself in a lighthearted way.

Don't make big long paragraphs. When someone looks at a long paragraph it looks like hard work. Also don't make sentences too long, people have to stop and think and then they could miss the point you are trying to make.

The first book I had published was, *"Living in the Supernatural."* It was published by Strang Communications in Lake Mary FL, about fifteen years ago. When I sent it in I was so happy because in a sense it was my baby. I didn't realize it at the time, but it represented me.

When they finished editing it they sent it back for approval before printing. There was about one third missing. I was so upset because what I said was really important. I called to ask why they taken out some of my stories. *"You said the same thing in three different chapters,"* the editor told me. But I didn't see it that way. I thought that my stories were good. They were good, but I had already gotten the point across in  the first chapter.

## Why are you writing?

Why are you writing or wanting to write? Is it to get out a message? Or tell your story? Or someone else's story? Or a fictional story? Is it about you, or is it about conveying a message in some form?

If you are writing and you are into you, the chances are that you won't reach people. If you are writing for others (and isn't that the purpose of a book in the first place?) you will touch your readers, providing you don't let what you are doing be lost in saying things in a complicated way.

## Getting Started

If you think about the whole, entire book you most probably will never start it. It will remain in your thought life. Your thoughts can be dismissed or they can bear fruit and transfer from your thoughts or your mind to a reality (an actual book of your own).

So, if you have a desire to write your story or teach some things, then there is a stage when you have to actually sit down at the computer and start. Most people think of the entire book and don't know where to begin or how to finish, so they never start it. But you don't have to have the whole thing or even know exactly how you are going to do it.

Just start and write the first thoughts that come to you. As you think of different things you want to say, then add them to your script. Keep a notebook or recorder near you all the time, because you can be in a store, driving your car, in a restaurant etc. and suddenly think of a story or a certain thing that you want to include.

When you get back to your computer put it in right away. I found sometimes that what I had in the beginning became the middle. It doesn't matter. You can sort it all out when you've finished. You can put it in order later.

Funny enough with each book I wrote I somehow knew it was the end and it was finished and there was nothing more to be said. That's how I am doing this small booklet to help you get started.

## Overcoming blockages

The term *"writer's cramp"* used to mean your hand was cramped through so much writing. It's hard for young people to imagine isn't it? Nowadays, people only seem to write by hand when they sign something.

These days you can get another kind of *"writer's cramp."* This is when you suddenly get what I call a "mind freeze." And it seems that suddenly the flow has stopped. This is the best thing that I have found to do. Sit down and write something. Anything!. Even if it doesn't seem to have anything to do with the book (you can always delete it later). But if you do that for a while it can unblock the pipe, so to speak.

# Finishing up

When you think about a cover - think about color. Color catches people's eye. You know how your eyes are drawn to color, you will pick something up because of it. Dark colors or what I call wishy-washy colors can actually push people away from a book,because unconsciously it has a negative effect. So be careful of that.

People like one-liners that make a statement. It sticks in their mind: i.e. *"It's OK to fall, but not to give up." "Negativism will prevent you from being a winner." "Don't let your past keep you from your future"* These can be dynamic and make great sub-headings or tag lines.

Some people have told me, *"I have several articles or books that I have started, but none of them finished."* So select the one thing you really want to say more than anything and concentrate on that one and FINISH it. Then you can go back to a second one.

Beware of Vanity Publishers. They will offer to edit, print, make a video and send out some flyers to advertise, and market your work so you can become successful. So they will print 3,000 or 4,000 books, but you have to pay (a lot), and it can cost as much as $10,000.00-$20,000.00

Most of the time you actually have to turn around and buy your books from them, after the initial free 100. If you're fortunate, you may be able to fly around the country doing book signings at bookstores and trade fares at you own expense and perhaps sell a few dozen books. But the amount of money you will make on your books sold through the publisher or distributor will probably be in cents, rather than dollars. This is why I am writing this to help you publish on a more realistic and attainable scale.

So you can step out in faith for the first 100 books. See what response you get; that's what I do. I write a booklet or article and send to it out to 200 people – and I wait to see what kind of response I get—Sometimes I think something is great, but it doesn't' "connect." So I forget it and maybe edit it and bring it out at a later date. This is the great thing about being able to do 10, 50 or 100 books; and then be able to change it for the next printing.

## Side note for overseas:

US AND EUROPE – We can have your books printed and shipped from US or the UK cutting costs significantly for you. We can also have them available on Kindle and Amazon and produce an e-Book for your own website. We will be happy to list your book on our website and direct people to you for sales.

For other countries we will format your book and have it ready for a printer in your country. We will assist you in finding a printer that will print your book at a price that will make it profitable for you.

You will receive the book in PDF format.

We hope you have fun. It's good to actually do something you've thought about for a long time. Even if you don't become a great, famous author, you will know you have accomplished something. And you never know what will happen with God, do you? And you never know who may read your book and be thoroughly blessed and helped.

I recently had some emails from people who live on an island I have never heard of, but they downloaded my books and CD's and were having a wonderful time in the Holy Spirit as a result.

You can also be a blessing to someone you may never meet personally through your message being out there!

We are also doing some children's story books and we will use the name of your son, daughter or grandchild as the hero

Kathie Walters
(with help and improvement from David Walters and Faith Walters)

For questions/help regarding your book email Faith at faithatgoodnews@gmail.com

My books and CD's are available on my website
www.kathiewaltersministry.com
Contact: kathiewalters@mindspring.com


David and Kathie Walters both minister out of
Good News Ministries in the United States and
overseas.
For further information write or call
GOOD NEWS MINISTRIES
220 Sleepy Creek Road • Macon, GA 31210
Web-site: www.kathiewaltersministry.com
Good News Ministries e-mail:
goodnewsministeries@usa.com
David's e-mail:
davidmwalters@mindspring.com
Kathie's e-mail:
kathiewalters@mindspring.com

# Other Books By David Walters

### KIDS IN COMBAT
Training children and youth to be radical for God.
For youth and children's pastors and parents.

### EQUIPPING THE YOUNGER SAINTS
A guide for teachers and parents on teaching children about
salvation and spiritual gifts.

### CHILDREN AFLAME
Amazing accounts of children from the journals of the great
Methodist preacher John Wesley in the 1700's and David's own
accounts with children and youth today.

### RADICAL LIVING IN A GODLESS SOCIETY
Our Godless society really targets our children and youth. How
do we cope with this situation?

### THE ANOINTING & YOU
*UNDERSTANDING REVIVAL*
What we must do to receive and impart the anointing & revival
to pass it on to the next generation.

### LIVING IN REVIVAL
*The Everyday Lifestyle Of The Normal  Christian*

God's intention for us through the power of His Holy Spirit. Diary
of Miraculous Events, Angelic visitations, freedom of the spirit,
Divine encounters, Deliverance, Healing, Prosperity and
Salvation.

## CHILDREN'S BIBLE STUDY BOOKS
## (ILLUSTRATED) FOR AGES 6–15
With Multiple-Choice Questions & Answers

### BEING A CHRISTIAN
A Bible study teaching children and teens how to be a Christian.

### FACT OR FANTASY?
A study on Christian Apologetics designed for children and youth.

### THE ARMOR OF GOD
A children's Bible study based on Ephesians 6:10–18.

### CHILDREN'S PRAYER MANUAL
Children's illustrated study on prayer

### FRUIT OF THE SPIRIT
A study teaching children and teens how to be a fruitful Christian.

### THE GIFTS OF THE SPIRIT
Children's illustrated Bible study on the gifts of the Spirit (ages 7 years–adult).

**Adventure Books For Youngsters.**
**By David Walters.**

### THE BOOK OF FUNTASTIC ADVENTURES
*Bedtime stories to make children & parents laugh* Eleven imaginary stories of David's two grandsons as Jedi knights having amazing hilarious adventures with Superheroes & story book characters.  Ages 8-14

### THE SECOND BOOK OF FUNTASTIC ADVENTURES
More hilarious adventures of David's two grandsons as Jedi Knights traveling through space with Moses their robot pilot searching for their parents and sister who have been kidnapped by aliens.
Ages 8-14

### THE ADVENTURES OF TINY THE BEAR
An amusing set of stories to help children deal with name calling and bullying. Ages 6-10

### HOW TO BE ORDINIARY, AVERAGE, MEDIOCRE & UNSUCESSFUL
An amusing reverse psychology booklet that says if you do the opposite to what this booklet proposes you may suffer the curse of success.

# Books By Kathie Walters

## ANGELS WATCHING OVER YOU
Did you know that angels are active in our everyday lives?

## THE BRIGHT AND SHINING REVIVAL
An account of the Hebrides Revival 1948–1952.

## CELTIC FLAMES
Read the exciting accounts of famous fourth- and fifth century Celtic Christians: Patrick, Brendan, and others.

## COLUMBA—THE CELTIC DOVE
Read about the ministry of this famous Celtic Christian, filled with supernatural visitations.

## PARENTING BY THE SPIRIT
The author shows how she raised her children by listening to the Holy Spirit rather than her emotions.

## LIVING IN THE SUPERNATURAL
How to live in our inheritance—supernaturally.

## THE SPIRIT OF FALSE JUDGMENT
In the light of holy revelation, sometimes things are different from what we perceive them to be.

## THE VISITATION
Supernatural visitations of a mother and daughter.

## PROGEST...WHAT?
Natural hormone replacement explained.

## "Holy Spirit Revival Encounters"

for the Whole Family

Pastors, Youth Pastors, Children's Pastors
Sunday School Teachers, Children's Workers, Nursery
Workers, Children, Teens, Single Adults, Parents,
Grandparents & Grandchildren.

The churches in your area can experience one of these dynamic Events. Author, speaker and revivalist, David Walters, imparts a fresh vision and anointing to everyone including those who work with children and youth. Walters says:

"Children do not have a baby or junior Holy Spirit!"

"Children are baptized in the Holy Spirit to do much more than play, be entertained or listen to a few moral object lessons!"

"The average church-wise child can be turned around and set on fire for God!"

"Christian teenagers do not have to surrender to peer pressure—they can become the peers!"

Families can be transformed.

## TOURS OF IRELAND AND SCOTLAND

with Kathie Walters

Come to Ireland and Scotland on a 10-Day Celtic Heritage Tour with Kathie Walters!

• Re-dig the spiritual wells of this beautiful country.

• Pray on the Hill of Slane where St. Patrick lit his Pascal fire and defied the High King.

• See the place where St. Patrick first landed to bring the Gospel to Ireland by God through the angel of Ireland, Victor.

• See the green hills and dales of Ireland—a picture you will never forget.

• Visit the ancient places of worship that will help enable you to grasp hold of your godly inheritance.

Then on to Scotland

• Tour the beautiful highlands of Scotland.

• Visit the island of Iona, where St. Columba built his monastery.

• Tour the Hebrides Islands. (Visit the church and talk to the people who were in the great revival there during 1949–1952.)

Made in the USA
Charleston, SC
28 March 2014